PAIRPOINT

LAMPS

Edward and Sheila
Malakoff

1469 Morstein Road, West Chester, Pennsylvania 19380

Acknowledgments

In the writing of this book help was always needed and gratefully accepted. But along with this help came support and encouragement from family and friends needed to fulfill our dream. We specifically wish to thank the following people:

Mr. Ronald Aiello
Mrs. Eleanor Carroll
Allan and Adele Grodsky
George Holmes of *Jewelers Circular Keystone*
Mrs. Carol Kahn
Mark and Marie Kaplan
Mrs. Isobel McKeown
Mr. Louis St. Albans, Jr.
Harvey and Eileen Weinstein

However much incentive these people provided, we would be remiss if we did not afford special mention to Mr. Peter Schiffer, our publisher, and Mr. Tim Scott, our photographer.

Printed in the United States of America.
ISBN: 0-88740-281-X

We are interested in hearing from authors with book ideas on related subjects.

Published by Schiffer Publishing, Ltd.
1469 Morstein Road
West Chester, Pennsylvania 19380
Please write for a free catalog.
This book may be purchased from the publisher.
Please include $2.00 postage.
Try your bookstore first.

Dedication

We dedicate this book to the present:

Dr. Gary Malakoff, our son
Ms. Lori Malakoff, our daughter
Dr. Susan Rattner, our daughter-in-law

and to the future:

Master Ian Seth Malakoff, our grandson.

Title page photo:
Puffy decoration on a Poppy shade that is 14 inches in diameter. There are various finishes on the signed base. The serial number is 3053.

Contents

Introduction

Mention New Bedford, Massachusetts, and a history buff immediately will respond, "whaling." If your listener is a literary buff, *Moby Dick* will come to mind. Should he be an antique collector, he might possibly think of Mount Washington Glass Company or the Pairpoint Corporation as leading names in one of America's most fascinating art industries. For over ninety years the New Bedford area was the home of glass manufacturing companies, the Pairpoint Corporation in particular.

Our original goal in producing this book was to provide a photographic panorama of this part of our American cultural heritage for today's ever-widening circle of collectors. Now it has expanded to a project wherein we hope to preserve the knowledge and the beauty of Pairpoint lamps for all art lovers to enjoy. In over forty years of traveling and antiquing, we have run the gamut, changing from eclectic collectors to one-item specialists. We love what we have and have what we love. The search for these rare and beautiful lamps has added as much excitement to our lives as the actual possession.

Opposite page:
Puffy Lilac tree shade,
signed, 14 inches in diameter.
Tree trunk base in two
finishes, signed. The serial
number is 3092.

Brief History

Between the years 1907 and 1929, when beauty in the home was highlighted by the wave of Art Nouveau, the Pairpoint Corporation added an innovative line to its already popular art glass, cut glass, and silver-plated products. The company chose not to be totally influenced by this stylized period. Their "electroliers" were a completely new and inventive art form. These mold-blown, reverse-painted lamps, enhanced by the invention of the electric light bulb, were introduced to the marketplace. In many prestigious outlets at home and abroad, Pairpoint lamps were sold at prices up to $125.00 each. More importantly, today this wholly American art form has taken its long-deserved place in history. Now, almost sixty years after their production has ceased, enthusiastic and discerning collectors have increased their value far beyond their creator's imaginations.

The corporation had sales offices at 43 West 23rd Street, New York; 402 Columbus Building, Chicago; 140 Geary Street, San Francisco; and Coristine Building, Montreal, Canada.

Time Line

1880-1894: Pairpoint Manufacturing Company (manufactured only silver).

July 14, 1894: Added glass products when taken over by Mount Washington Glass Company.

1900-1938: Reorganized as Pairpoint Corporation.

1939-1952: Gundersen Glass.

1952-1957: Gundersen Pairpoint Glass.

October 2, 1965: Fire destroyed the old Pairpoint factory and with it over 100 years of New Bedford glass manufacturing.

Puffy Orange Tree shade
with oranges and a butterfly
on green leafy branches. The
shade is 14 inches in
diameter. Tree trunk base,
signed, in two finishes. The
serial number is 3092.

Glass Shades

Over a period spanning more than twenty years, the Pairpoint Corporation produced many lamps with shades of varying sizes, shapes, and materials. Although parchment, metal, and cut glass shades were produced, the mold-blown glass shades were the most popular. Every Pairpoint shade was made by the company itself.

As collectors, we have classified these shades into several categories: scenics, puffies, ribbed, metal, floor lamps, chandeliers, and nonelectric candle lamps.

Lamp shade diameters range from the smallest four-inch miniature to the largest twenty-inch scenic. Often, many variations of the same-shaped shade were painted depending on customer's requests. Changing a background color or a painted hue gave two of the same molds quite a different impression.

All glass shades were acidized (frosted) prior to being decorated. Because they were reverse painted, most shades have retained their original color. Even though these glass shades were mold-blown, no mold marks are visible. This is due to a unique process of lining the mold with beeswax and then fire-polishing the shade.

Every Pairpoint shade that left the factory was stamped on the lower inside or outside edge with one of the following four markings: 1) The Pairpoint Corporation; 2) Patented July 9, 1907; 3) Patent Pending; 4) Patent Applied For.

The scenic shades were occasionally signed by the artist when he or she was particularly pleased with an exceptional work. Some of the artists included Frank Guba, H. Fisher, Adolph Frederick (aka C. Durand), Roe Tripp, W. Macy, L. Anna, L. Fisher, and C. Bradley. As a tribute to the skill of these artists, the decoration of one medium-sized Pairpoint shade should be equated to the work required to paint a twenty-by-forty-inch canvas. The puffies were never signed by an artist since they were the product of more than one person.

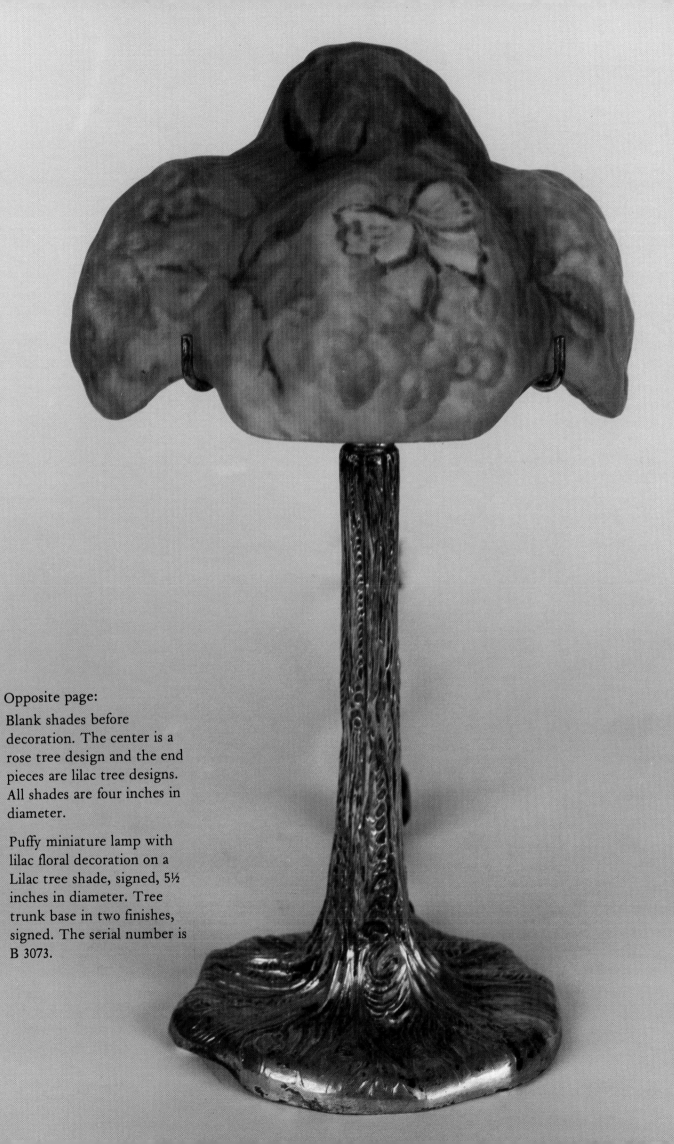

Opposite page:

Blank shades before decoration. The center is a rose tree design and the end pieces are lilac tree designs. All shades are four inches in diameter.

Puffy miniature lamp with lilac floral decoration on a Lilac tree shade, signed, 5½ inches in diameter. Tree trunk base in two finishes, signed. The serial number is B 3073.

9

Bases

Finishes of bronze, brass, silver plate, copper, as well as glass and mahogany were some of the materials used to make the bases. All bases were signed "THE PAIRPOINT CORPORATION" along with the logo, ⬦P⬦ the letter "P" inside a diamond, impressed (signed) on the underside of the base. A style number also appeared. Thomas J. Pairpoint, the first superintendent of the company, instituted this logo on October 1, 1880.

The Pairpoint Corporation suffered business losses in 1929 and was forced to close its doors. The glass works have since been reopened sporadically under different managements, different names, and in different locations. However, these lamps never again appeared on the production line.

Styles

Another view of lamp on page 7.

Puffy gray and white snow owl. Owl shade, signed, 10 inches in diameter. Owl base, signed, in two finishes. The serial number is 3090.

Puffy brown barn owl with
an Owl shade, signed, 10
inches in diameter. Owl base,
signed, in two finishes. The
serial number is 3090.

Puffy, darker variation of other apple tree with an Apple tree shade, signed, 12 inches in diameter. Tree trunk base, signed, in two finishes. The serial number is 3092.

Inset on previous page:
Puffy and blown out lamp
with apple blossoms, apples,
bumblebees, butterfly, and
green leaves. Apple tree
shade, signed, 12 inches in
diameter. Base is a two-color
tree trunk, signed. The serial
number is 3092.

Begonia shade, signed, 16
inches in diameter. Signed
base with two finishes. The
serial number is B 3020.

16

Multicolored grapes on a grape base. Puffy Grape shade, signed, 12 inches in diameter. Signed grape base in two finishes. The serial number is 3089.

Puffy red poppies in a green
background on a signed
Poppy shade, 12 inches in
diameter. The base is signed,
in two finishes. The serial
number is 3047.

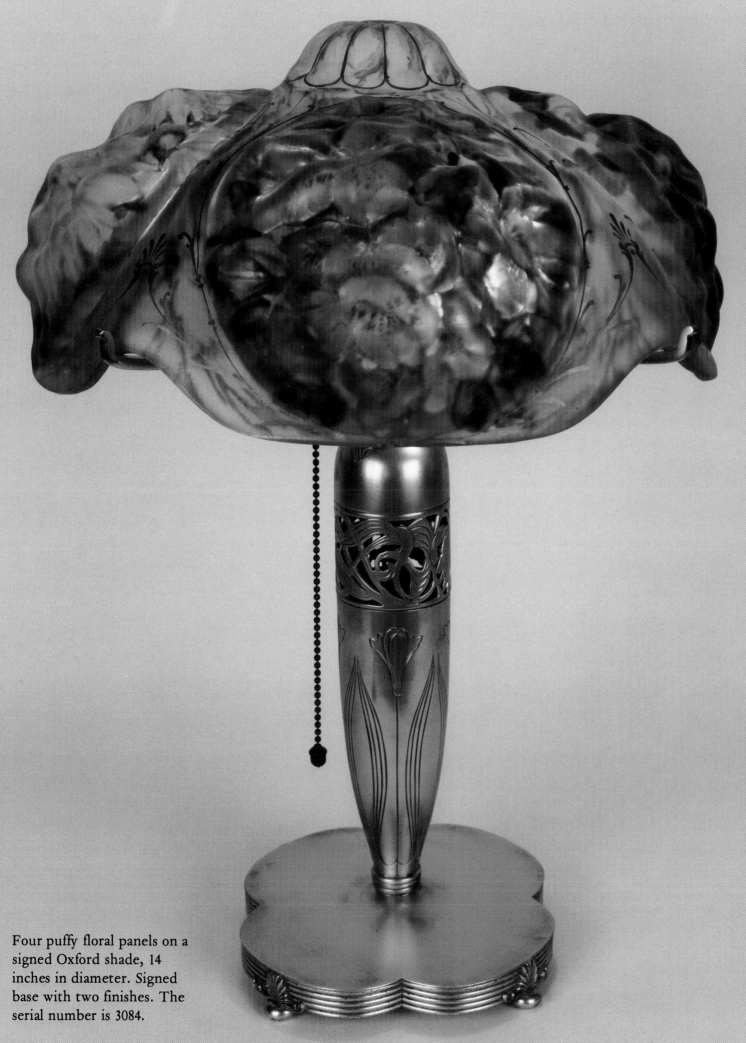

Four puffy floral panels on a
signed Oxford shade, 14
inches in diameter. Signed
base with two finishes. The
serial number is 3084.

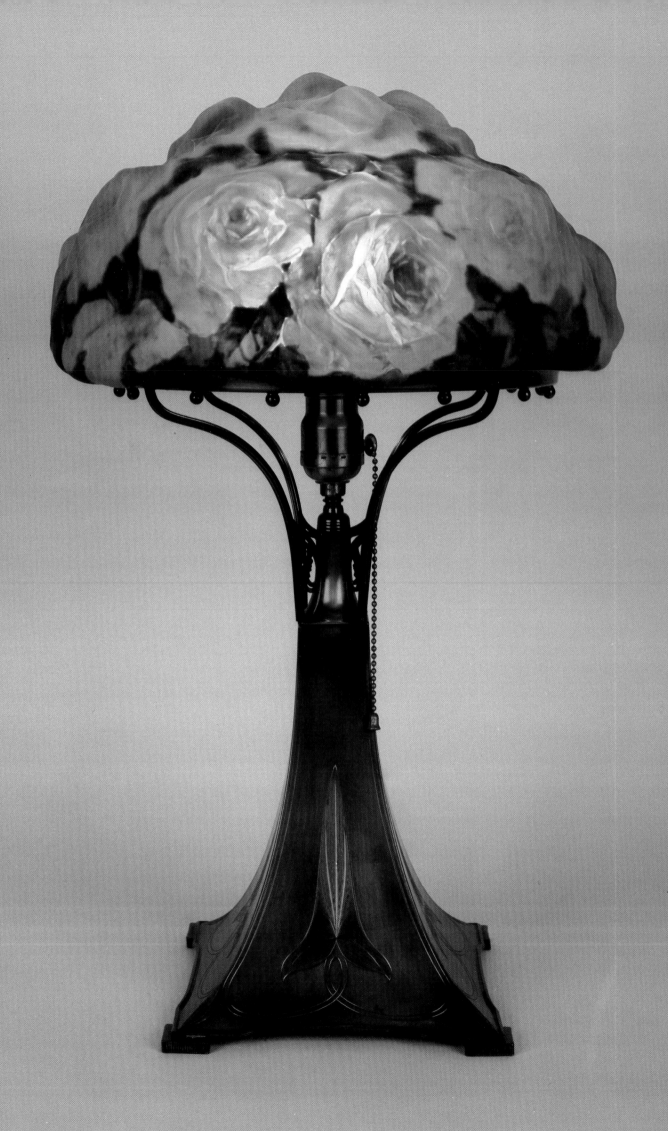

Square lamp featuring Albemarl shade with roses and butterflies and an open top. Shade is 12 inches wide. The base is signed, in four finishes. The serial number is B 3099.

Opposite page:

Puffy yellow roses on a Rose shade, signed, ten inches in diameter. Signed base with two finishes. The serial number is 3052.

Puffy with clusters of lilacs and foliage on a signed Palermo shade, 16 inches in diameter. Signed base in two finishes. The serial number is B 3099.

Four butterflies, red and
pink with rose border.
Papillon shade, signed, 14
inches in diameter. The base
is signed and has varying
finishes. The serial number is
C 3066.

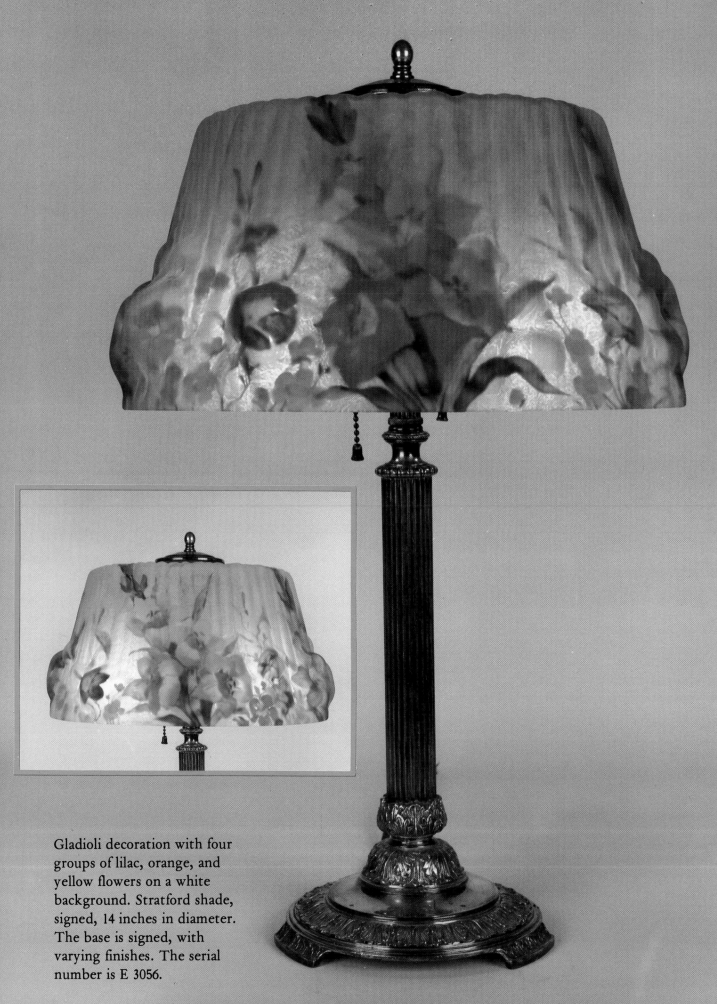

Gladioli decoration with four groups of lilac, orange, and yellow flowers on a white background. Stratford shade, signed, 14 inches in diameter. The base is signed, with varying finishes. The serial number is E 3056.

24

Apple blossoms and roses on
a San Remo shade that is
puffy and blown out on two
sides. The shade is signed
and 12 inches wide. The base
is signed, in four finishes.
The serial number is B 3034.

Iris blossoms and varicolored flowers on a signed Iris blossom shade, 16 inches in diameter. Signed base in two finishes. The serial number is 3066.

Open top with garlands of apple blossoms, roses, daisies. Soft yellow background. Marlborough shade, signed, 14 inches in diameter. The base is in two finishes and is signed. The serial number is B 3020.

Chrysanthemums and
hummingbird decoration on
a signed Stratford shade, 14
inches in diameter. Signed
base with two finishes. The
serial number is C 3066.

Tulips on a turquoise background, puffed out on two sides. Roma shade, signed, 13 inches wide. The base is signed, in four finishes. The serial number is 3093½.

Pink background with dogwoods and hummingbird in Coralline finish on a signed Stratford shade, 16 inches in diameter. The base has two finishes and is signed. The serial number is D 3070.

Iris decoration on a signed
Stratford shade, 14 inches in
diameter. There are various
finishes on the signed base.
The serial number is B 3030.

Hummingbird and floral decoration with green stripes on a signed Stratford shade, 14 inches in diameter. Two finishes on the signed base. The serial number is B 3055½.

Floral garlands decorate this signed Devonshire shade that is 16 inches in diameter. The base has two finishes and is signed. The serial number is B 3056.

Puffy signed Iris shade, 16
inches in diameter. Two
finishes on the signed base.
The serial number is B 3056.

Butterflies and apple
blossoms on a signed Papillon
shade, 16 inches in diameter.
Signed base, in two finishes.
The serial number is C 3066.

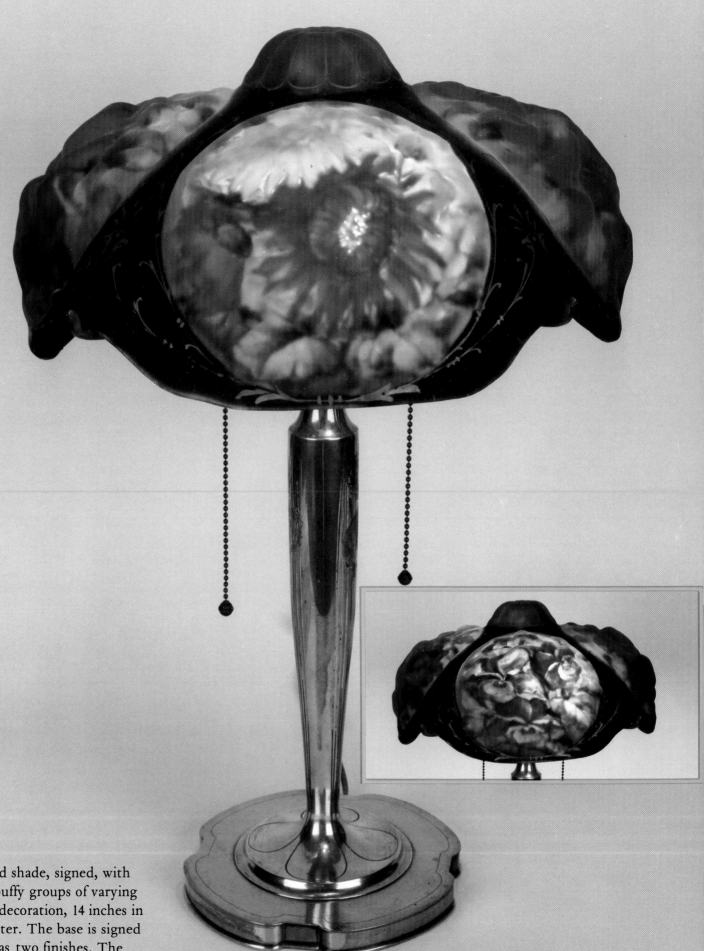

Oxford shade, signed, with
four puffy groups of varying
floral decoration, 14 inches in
diameter. The base is signed
and has two finishes. The
serial number is B 3012.

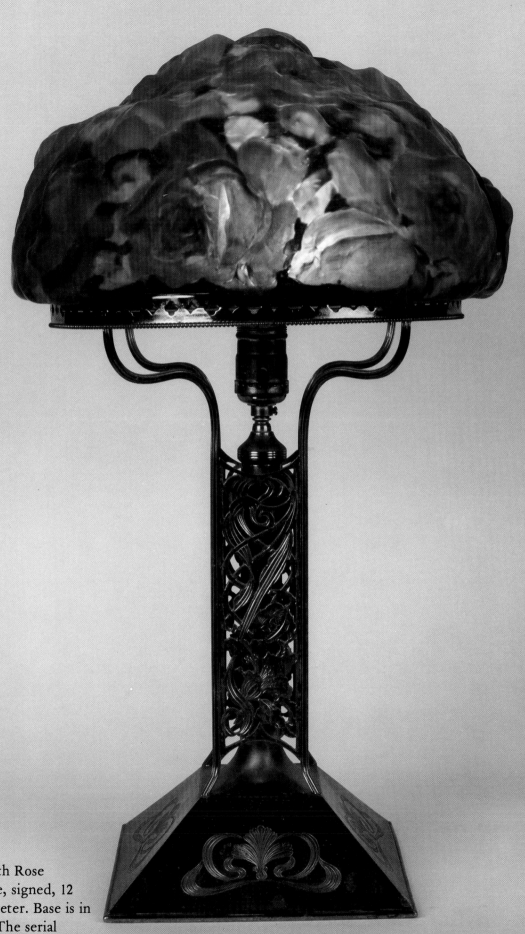

Puffy lamp with Rose
Bouquet shade, signed, 12
inches in diameter. Base is in
four finishes. The serial
number is 3047.

Butterflies and roses on a
dark green background (with
shades in the varied
background). Signed Papillon
shade, 14 inches in diameter.
The base is signed, in four
finishes. The serial number is
B 3029.

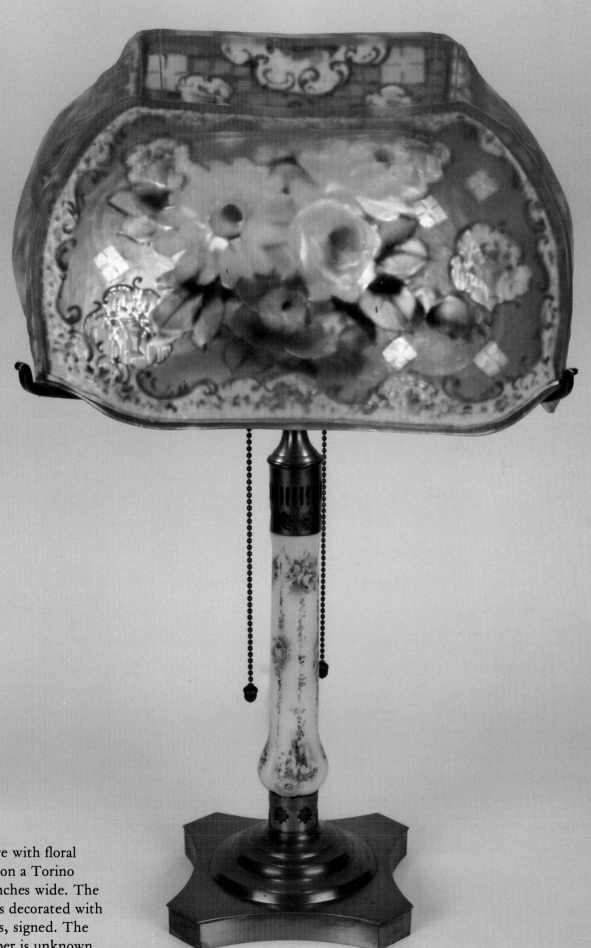

Puffy square with floral decoration on a Torino shade, 14 inches wide. The base is glass decorated with two finishes, signed. The serial number is unknown.

Signed Grape shade with
leaves with open top. There
are two finishes on the
signed base. The serial
number is B 3010.

Hummingbird and flowers in
Coralline finish on a signed
Stratford shade, 14 inches in
diameter. The base has two
finishes and is signed. The
serial number is D 3066.

Puffy roses on a signed Rose
Bouquet shade, 14 inches in
diameter. The signed base
has two finishes. The serial
number is 3055.

Puffy, assorted azalea bouquet on an Azalea Bouquet shade, signed, 14 inches in diameter. Flower pot base in various finishes, signed. The serial number is unknown.

Puffy signed Stratford shade with varicolored gladioli, 14 inches in diameter. Signed base, in two finishes. The serial number is E 3056.

44

Hummingbirds and roses on a puffy, 15-inch-diameter signed Devonshire shade with various backgrounds. The base is signed, in four finishes. The serial number is B 3055½.

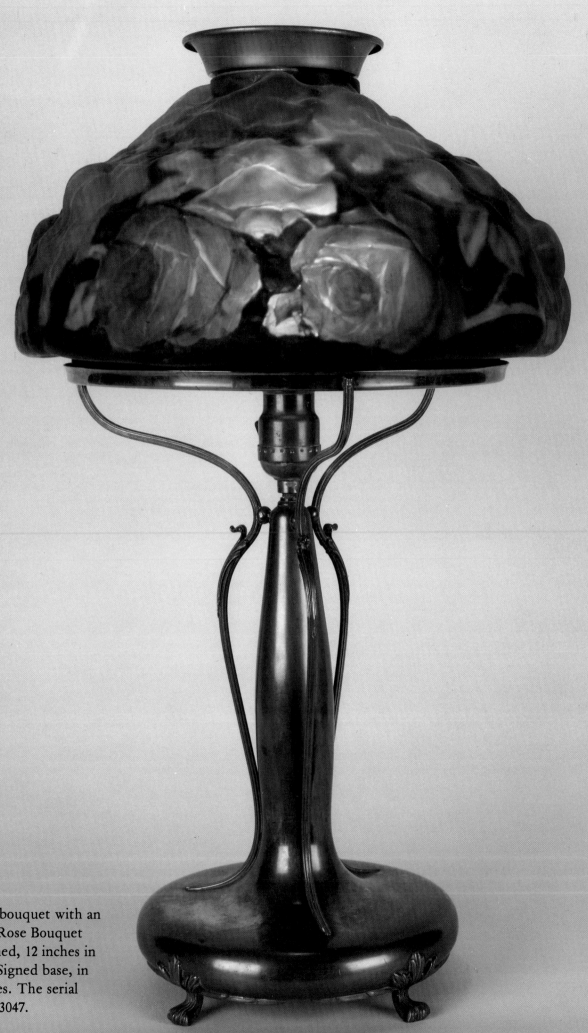

Puffy rose bouquet with an
open top. Rose Bouquet
shade, signed, 12 inches in
diameter. Signed base, in
four finishes. The serial
number is 3047.

Puffy signed Stratford shade, 14 inches in diameter, with hummingbirds and roses. The base is signed, in two finishes. The serial number is C 3066.

Puffy roses adorn a signed
Rose Bouquet shade that is
14 inches in diameter. Rose
tree base. The serial number
is 3095.

Puffy white roses and
hummingbird in pink
background on a signed
Devonshire shade that is 16
inches in diameter. Gold tree
trunk base, signed. The
serial number is 3092.

Garland of flowers are
featured on this signed
Devonshire shade, 16 inches
in diameter. The base has
two finishes and is signed.
The serial number is 3093.

Open top signed Oxford
shade with four puffy groups
of varying floral decoration.
The shade is 14 inches in
diameter; the base has two
finishes and is signed. The
serial number is B 3033.

Butterflies and roses on a
signed 16-inch-diameter
Papillon shade with a closed
top. Signed base in four
finishes. The serial number is
B 3020.

Floral puffy garlands are
featured on a signed Ravenna
shade, 14 inches in diameter.
There are two finishes on the
signed base. The serial
number is unknown.

Multicolored roses adorn a
signed Rose Bouquet shade,
ten inches in diameter. The
base is signed; the serial
number is 3093½.

Puffy Chestnut shade,
signed, 12 inches in diameter,
with floral design. The
mahogany base is signed; the
serial number is C 3095.

Puffy signed Pansy shade with open top. The shade is 14 inches in diameter and also was made with closed top and various colors. The base has two finishes and is signed. The serial number is B 3066.

Puffy Lotus shade, ten inches in diameter. Signed base with two finishes. The serial number is 3053.

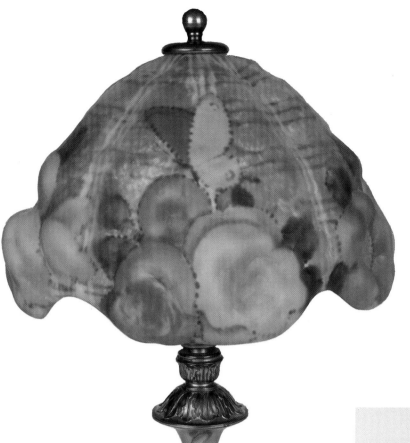

Opposite page:
Puffy roses on two sides and geometric design on two sides of this signed Ravenna shade, which is ten inches wide. Signed base in two finishes. The serial number is B 3051.

Puffy boudoir with rose border, butterfly, and lattice decoration. Rose tree shade, signed, eight inches in diameter. Signed base in two finishes. The serial number is E 3055.

Puffy boudoir lamp with dogwood blossoms and butterflies. Papillon shade, signed, eight inches in diameter. The base is signed and in two finishes. The serial number is C 3057.

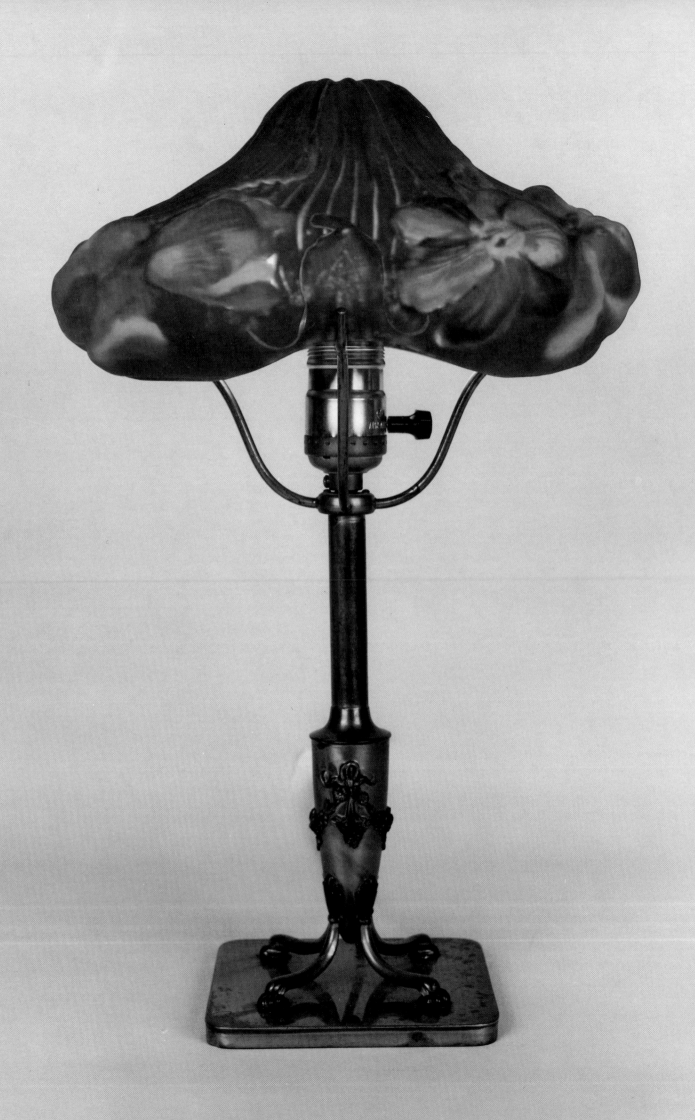

Puffy boudoir lamp with floral border and lattice decoration on a signed Stratford shade, eight inches in diameter. The base is signed and in two finishes. The serial number is C 3057.

Opposite page:
Puffy, signed Tulip shade featuring four-color tulip decoration. The shade is eight inches in diameter. The brass base is signed; the serial number is B 3025.

Puffy boudoir with black border and dogwood blossoms on a signed Stratford shade, eight inches in diameter. There are two finishes on the signed base. The serial number is C 3064.

Puffy boudoir lamp with chrysanthemum border decoration. The signed Stratford shade is eight inches in diameter. The base is signed and in two finishes. The serial number is C 3076.

Puffy roses are featured on a signed Bonnet shade, eight inches in diameter. The base has two finishes and is signed. The serial number is C 3023.

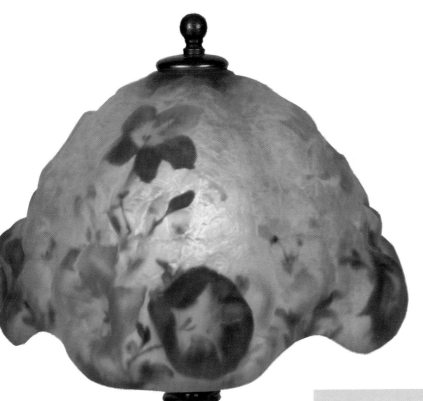

Puffy boudoir lamp with pansy border on a Pansy tree shade, signed, eight inches in diameter. The base is signed and in two finishes. The serial number is D 3022.

Puffy, signed Stratford shade with apple blossoms and roses on a black border. The shade is eight inches in diameter. Mahogany base, signed. The serial number is C 3093.

Puffy boudoir lamp with dogwood blossoms and black border on a signed Stratford shade, eight inches in diameter. The base is signed and in two finishes. The serial number is C 3064.

Puffy Portsmouth shade on a boudoir lamp with four panels of flowers. The shade is signed and eight inches in diameter. There are two finishes on the signed base. The serial number is B 3051.

Roses and butterflies on a puffy boudoir lamp with a signed Papillon shade, eight inches in diameter. The base is signed and in two finishes. The serial number is C 3064.

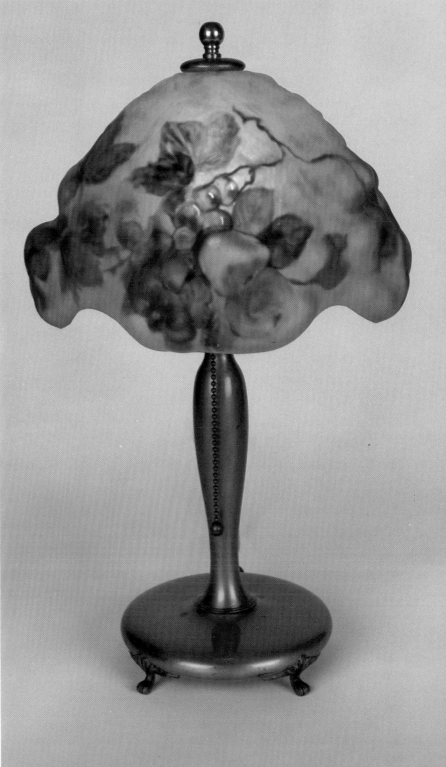

Puffy boudoir lamp with mixed fruit border. Fruit tree shade, signed, eight inches in diameter. Signed base in two finishes. The serial number is 3047½.

Puffy lamp with signed Pansy shade, 5½ inches in diameter. Signed tree trunk base in two finishes. The serial number is B 3073.

Opposite page:
Four groups of varicolored gladioli. Signed Stratford shade, eight inches in diameter. The base is signed, in two finishes. The serial number is C 3064.

Dogwood flowers in Coralline finish on a signed Stratford shade, eight inches in diameter. Signed tree trunk base. The serial number is 3079.

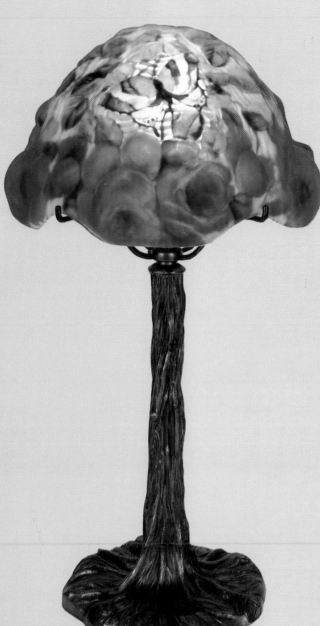

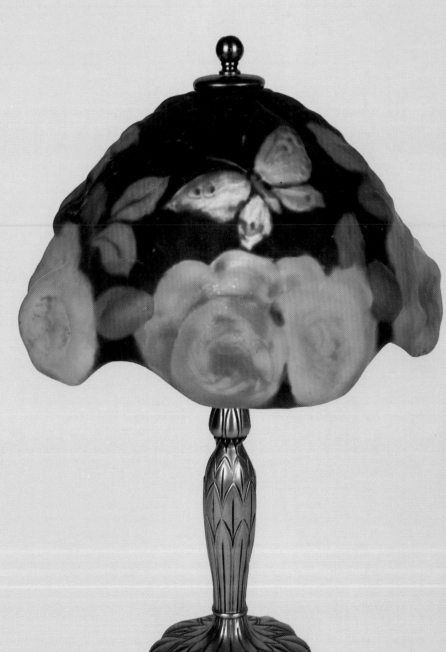

Opposite page:

Puffy miniature lamps with butterflies and roses. Puffy Floral shades, signed, five inches in diameter. The base is signed and in two finishes. The serial number on the left lamp is 3046; the right lamp is B 6171.

Rose tree shade, eight inches in diameter. Tree trunk base in two finishes, signed. The serial number is B 3078.

Puffy boudoir lamp with roses and butterflies. Rose tree shade, signed, eight inches in diameter. Signed base in two finishes. The serial number is C 3064.

Puffy lamp with Pansy shade and closed top and rare dark background. The shade is signed and is three inches in diameter. The base is in two finishes and signed. The serial number is 3080.

Puffy dogwood flowers sitting on a spider. Dogwood shade, signed, 5½ inches in diameter. Signed mahogany base. The serial number is C 3085.

Puffy Balmoral shade featuring daisies and butterflies on a multicolored background. The shade is signed and five inches in diameter. Tree trunk base in two finishes, signed. The serial number is B 3073.

Puffy Rose tree shade with roses on rare black background. The shade is signed and five inches in diameter. Signed tree trunk base in two finishes. The serial number is B 3073.

Puffy lamp with roses on a signed Windsor shade with open top, five inches in diameter. Tree trunk base, signed, in two finishes. The serial number is B 3073.

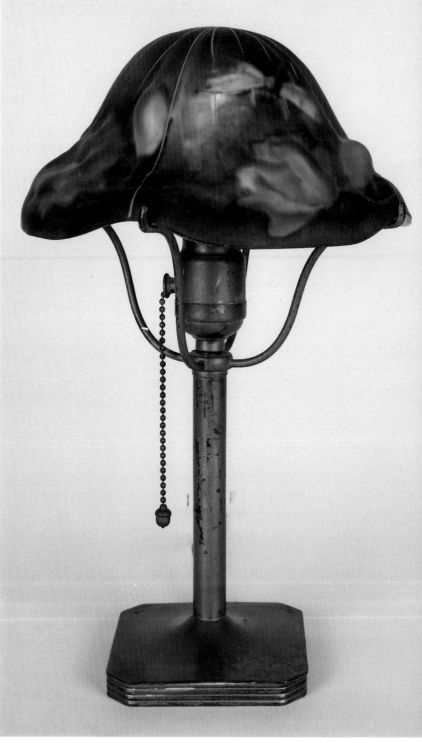

Boudoir lamp with dragonfly and four-inch-diameter Tivoli shade. The base has two finishes and is signed. The serial number is B 3022.

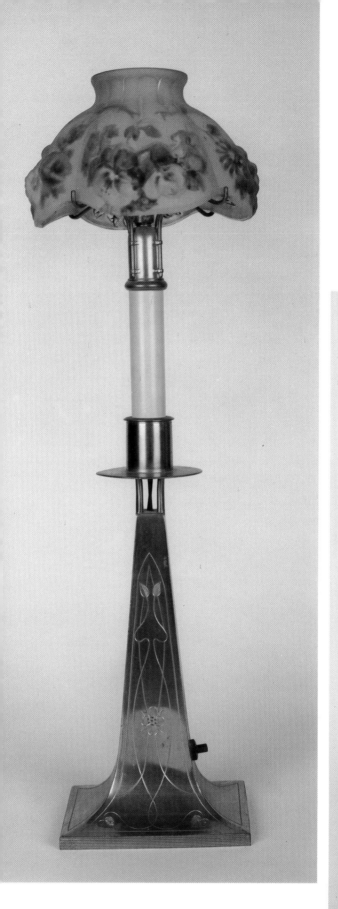

Puffy lamp with six-inch-diameter shade featuring floral decoration. Candlestick base, signed, in two finishes. The serial number is B 6150.

Puffy roses on a rare black background of this Rose Bonnet shade, which is signed and five inches in diameter. The base is a signed tree trunk in two finishes. The serial number is B 3073.

Grapes and open top are featured on a signed four-inch-diameter Grape shade. The base has two finishes and is signed. The serial number is D 3034½.

Boudoir lamp with open top and mixed florals. Signed Concord shade, five inches in diameter. The base has two finishes and is signed. The serial number is C 3064.

Dragonfly and floral
decoration on a signed
Boudoir shade, four inches in
diameter. Signed base, in
two finishes. The serial
number is B 3021.

Puffy dragonfly and floral
decoration on a signed Tivoli
shade, eight inches in
diameter. The base is signed
and in two finishes. The
serial number is C 3076.

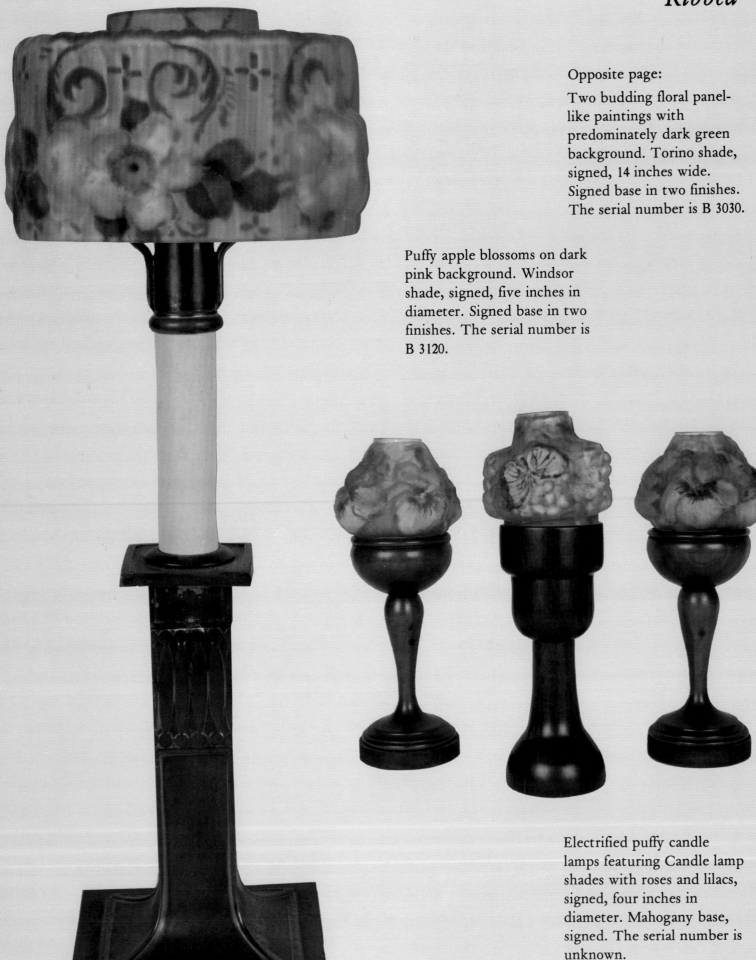

Ribbed

Opposite page:

Two budding floral panel-like paintings with predominately dark green background. Torino shade, signed, 14 inches wide. Signed base in two finishes. The serial number is B 3030.

Puffy apple blossoms on dark pink background. Windsor shade, signed, five inches in diameter. Signed base in two finishes. The serial number is B 3120.

Electrified puffy candle lamps featuring Candle lamp shades with roses and lilacs, signed, four inches in diameter. Mahogany base, signed. The serial number is unknown.

Octagonal shape featuring
French fishing boats and
lighthouse. Malta shade,
signed, 14 inches in diameter.
The base is signed. The
serial number is C 3014.

Four panels featuring Venetian canal scenes, with blown out and ribbed Pisa shade that is signed and 16 inches wide. The base is signed. The serial number is B 2065.

Peach lacy design on a Lucca
shade, signed, 16 inches in
diameter. Signed base in four
finishes. The serial number is
B 3012.

Four panels of purple lilacs
connected by draperylike
glass corners, blown out and
ribbed. Pisa shade, signed, 14
inches wide. The base is
signed, in two finishes. The
serial number is B 2065.

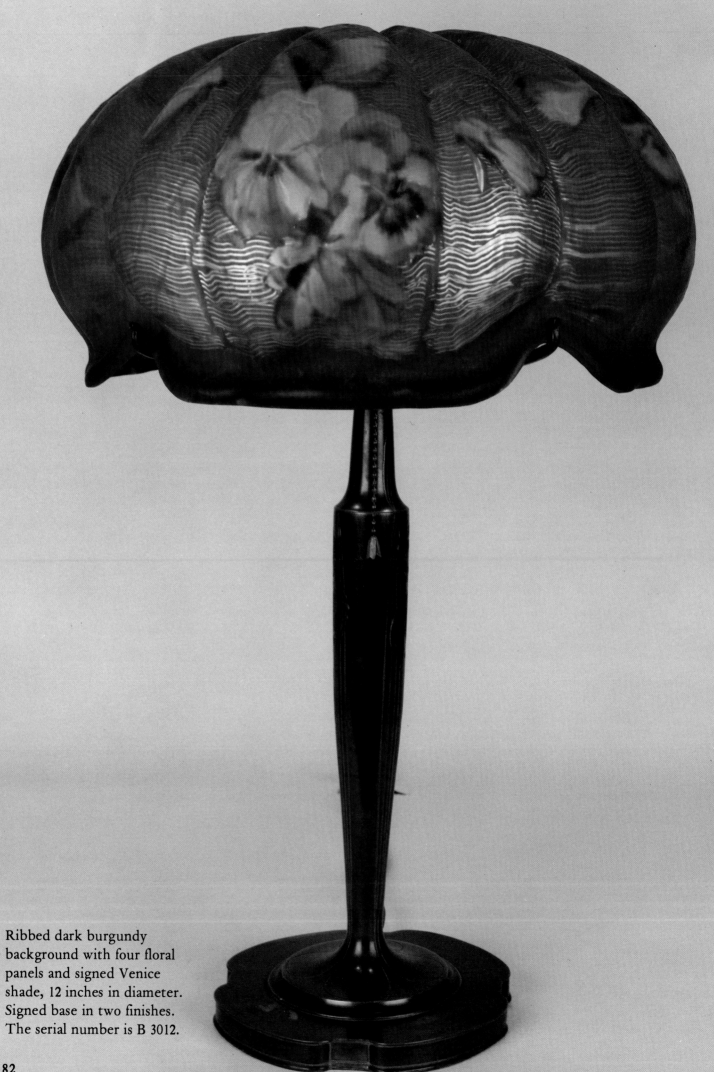

Ribbed dark burgundy
background with four floral
panels and signed Venice
shade, 12 inches in diameter.
Signed base in two finishes.
The serial number is B 3012.

Signed Palm shade, 14 inches in diameter. The base has various finishes and is signed. The serial number is B 3019.

Puffy with two nautical scenes on a signed Pompeii shade that is ten inches wide. The base is signed, in two finishes. The serial number is B 3050.

Square lamp with floral
decoration and 16-inch-wide
signed Pisa shade. Glass-
decorated base with two
finishes, signed. The serial
number is C 3005.

Ribbed green background
with large pink floral
decoration. Venice shade,
signed, 12 inches in diameter.
Signed base in two finishes.
The serial number is B 3019.

Green garlands and flowers
on a signed Murano shade.
Signed mahogany base. The
serial number is D 3009.

Flamingoes with a bright, sunny background. Danver shade, signed, 20 inches in diameter. Signed base in two finishes. The serial number is D 3026½.

Venetian harbor with ribbed and open top. Chesterfield shade, signed, 14 inches in diameter. Signed tree trunk base in two finishes. The serial number is 3092.

Hexagonally shaped country lake scene on a signed Malta shade, 16 inches in diameter. The base is signed and in two finishes. The serial number is C 3063.

90

Venetian scene on a signed
Torino shade, 16 inches in
diameter. There are two
finishes on the signed base.
The serial number is 3088.

Pink lacy design on a signed
Tuscano shade, 16 inches in
diameter. Signed base in two
finishes. The serial number is
C 3063.

Chesterfield shade featuring
a floral design with a red
rose, signed, 16 inches in
diameter. Signed base in two
finishes. The serial number is
C 3037.

Ribbed Garden of Allah
scene with signed
Chesterfield shade, 14 inches
in diameter. The base is
signed, in two finishes. The
serial number is B 3030.

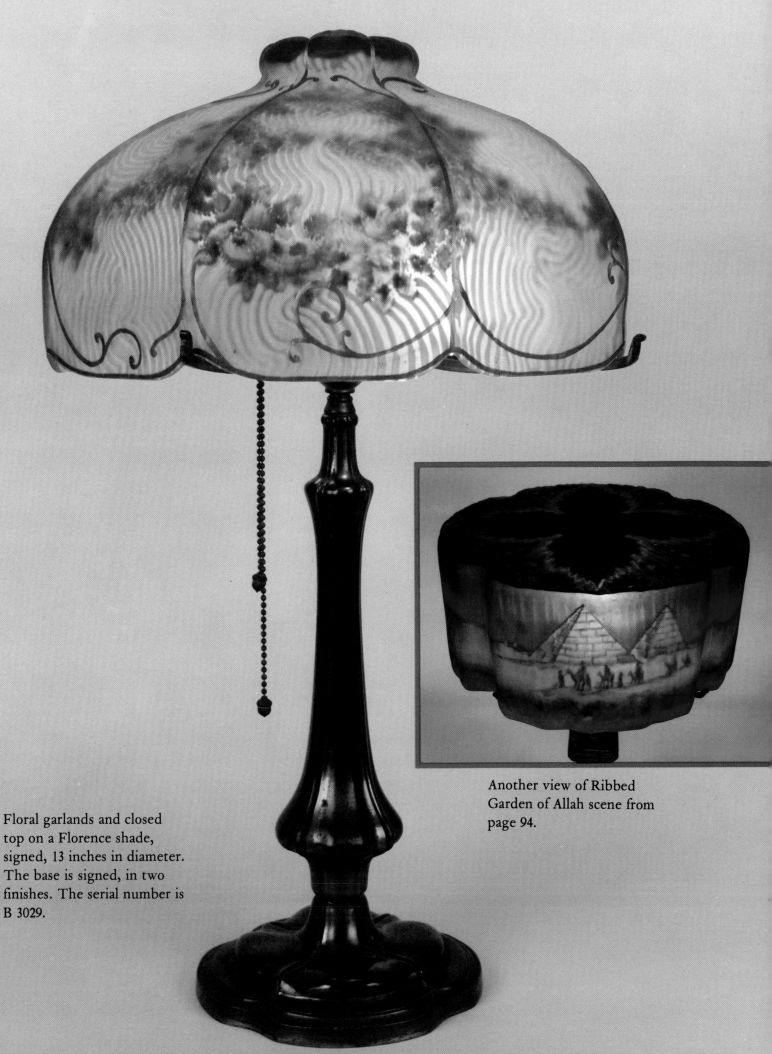

Floral garlands and closed
top on a Florence shade,
signed, 13 inches in diameter.
The base is signed, in two
finishes. The serial number is
B 3029.

Another view of Ribbed
Garden of Allah scene from
page 94.

Six panels of poppies on a
signed 12-inch-diameter
Venice shade with an open
top. Signed base in two
finishes. The serial number is
D 3095.

Red rose on a signed Venice
shade, 12 inches in diameter.
The base is signed and has
two finishes. The serial
number is C 3020.

Floral pattern on a burgundy
background. Tivoli shade,
signed, 16 inches in diameter.
Signed base in four finishes.
The serial number is C 3063.

Countryside scene on a
signed Palm shade, 14 inches
in diameter. Tree trunk
base, signed. The serial
number is 3091.

Fleur-de-lis design on white background on a signed Mozart shade, ten inches in diameter. Signed base in two finishes. The serial number is E 3055.

Boudoir lamp with Japanese peach blossoms on a signed Danver shade, eight inches in diameter. The base is signed and in two finishes. The serial number is D 3024½.

Miniature fleur-de-lis design on a white background. Signed Manchester shade, five inches in diameter. The base is signed and in two finishes. The serial number is C 3064.

Puffy lamp with signed Banana tree shade, five inches in diameter. Rare potted tree base, signed, in three finishes. The serial number is B 3086.

Butterfly and daisy
decoration on a signed
Balmoral shade, five inches in
diameter. Tree trunk base in
two finishes, signed. The
serial number is B 3073.

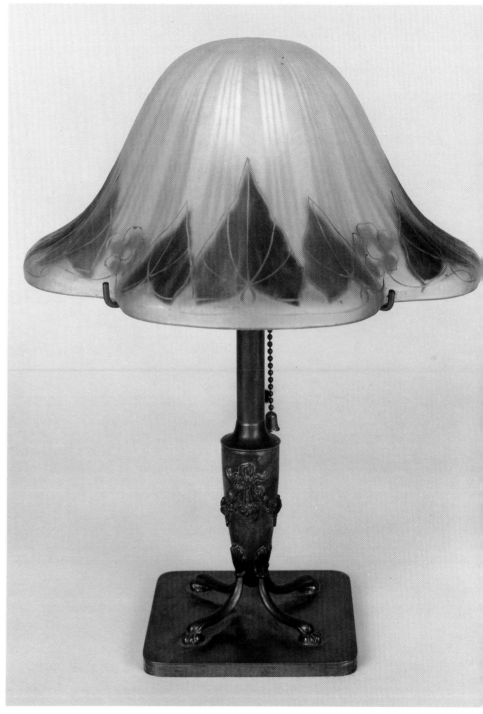

Puffy signed Palm shade, five
inches in diameter, with
garlands of flowers. The base
is signed and in two finishes.
The serial number is 3078.

Boudoir lamp with leaf
design border and gold
outline on exterior. Tivoli
shade, signed, ten inches in
diameter. The base is signed
and in two finishes. The
serial number is B 3025.

Spanish galleon on heavy
seas. Lansdowne shade,
signed, 16 inches in diameter.
Dolphin base, signed, with
two finishes. The serial
number is D 3076½.

New Bedford harbor scene.
Bombay shade, signed, 20
inches in diameter. The base
is signed and in two finishes.
The serial number is D 3059.

Four panels with nautical theme. Shade in Exeter pattern, signed, 17 inches in diameter. Dolphin base with two finishes, signed. The serial number is D 3076½.

Whaling ships on open seas
with Lansdowne shade,
signed, 16 inches in diameter.
Dolphin base, signed, with
two finishes. The serial
number is D 3076½.

Hexagonal lamp with nautical theme. Directoire shade, signed, 14 inches wide. Base is made of onyx and marble, signed. The serial number is E 3010.

Opposite page:
Venetian harbor scene on a
signed Carlisle shade signed
by F. Guba, 18 inches in
diameter. The base is signed
and in two finishes. The
serial number is D 3042.

Harbor scene on a signed
Lansdowne shade, 14 inches
in diameter. Signed base in
two finishes. The serial
number is D 3062.

Crows perched on vividly
flowering tree branch. Seville
shade, signed, 14 inches in
diameter. Signed base in two
finishes. The serial number is
D 3075.

Floral and bird design and Exeter shade, signed, 14 inches in diameter. Base is signed, in two finishes. The serial number is D 3041.

Parrots on a perch with a
blue background with a
signed Seville shade that is 15
inches in diameter. Signed
Brass and onyx base. The
serial number is D 3095.

Opposite page:
Two peacocks on a garden wall with a signed Carlisle shade, 16 inches in diameter. Signed base, in two finishes. The serial number is D 3084.

Black background and floral design with birds. Exeter shade, signed, 16 inches in diameter. The base is signed, in two finishes. The serial number is D 3084.

Floral design with birds on a Touraine shade, signed, 14 inches in diameter. Signed base, in two finishes. The serial number is D 3075.

113

Seascape and New England village featuring Vienna shade, signed, 14 inches in diameter. Planter base ring holder in two finishes, signed. The serial number is C 3072.

Dark green background with butterflies and Coralline finish on the exterior. Springfield shade, signed, 16 inches in diameter. The base is signed, in two colors, and the serial number is 3092.

New England country scene on a signed Seville shade, 16 inches in diameter. Signed base in two finishes. The serial number is D 3070.

116

Four panels, with one season featured on each panel. Exeter shade, signed, 20 inches in diameter. Signed base in two finishes. The serial number is D 3051.

Garden of Allah scene on a Carlisle shade, signed, 18 inches in diameter. Signed base in four finishes. The serial number is D 3042.

Floral with black enamel
outline painted on the
outside of this signed
Springfield shade, 16 inches
in diameter. Tree trunk base
in two finishes, signed. The
serial number is 3092.

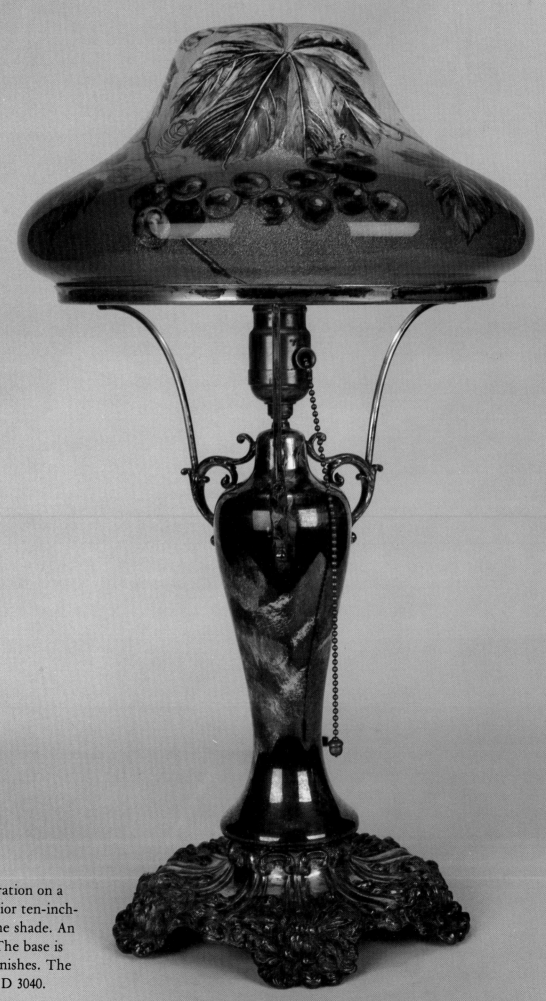

Grapevine decoration on a
satin glaze exterior ten-inch-
diameter Cologne shade. An
early example. The base is
signed, in two finishes. The
serial number is D 3040.

Floral print with black
enamel outline on the
exterior, featuring a
Springfield shade that is
signed and 16 inches in
diameter. Signed base in
various finishes. The serial
number is 3052½.

English forest and
countryside presented on a
signed Carlisle shade, 20
inches in diameter. Signed
base in four finishes. The
serial number is D 3053.

122

Farm scene on a signed 20-
inch-diameter Lansdowne
shade. The base is signed, in
two finishes. The serial
number is D 3059.

Sea gull nautical scene on matching signed glass base. Signed Copely shade, 20 inches in diameter. The serial number is D 3000.

124

Farm scene with all paint on the exterior, which is very rare. Carlisle shade, signed, 20 inches in diameter. Signed base, in six finishes. The serial number is D 3051.

Green Tivoli shade with
flowers, signed, 16 inches in
diameter. Pottery base made
by Hampshire for Pairpoint
Corporation. The serial
number is 6100.

126

Maple leaf design with black
enamel outline on the
exterior and crystal prisms
on the rim of the signed 16-
inch-diameter Springfield
shade. Signed base in two
finishes. The serial number is
B 3053½.

127

Hexagonal lamp with signed Directoire shade featuring tapestry panels, 14 inches wide. The signed base has two finishes. The serial number is E 3001.

Dutch landscape with Touraine shade that is signed, 12 inches in diameter. Signed mahogany base. The serial number is D 3008½.

Floral design with black
enamel outline on the
exterior. Vienna shade,
signed, ten inches in
diameter. Signed base in two
finishes. The serial number is
B 3008.

Forest scene with deer on a
signed Berkeley shade, 18
inches in diameter. Signed
base in three finishes. The
serial number is D 3070.

Grazing sheep farm scene on a signed Vienna shade, 14 inches in diameter. Planter base, signed, in two finishes. The serial number is C 3072.

Multicolored design with birds and flowers on a signed Carlisle shade, 18 inches in diameter. Signed base in two finishes. The serial number is D 3070.

Early example featuring matte finish, black enamel outline on the exterior. Signed Berlin shade is 12 inches in diameter. The base is signed and in two finishes. The serial number is 3039.

131

Sailing ships at sea at sunset
on a Lansdowne shade,
signed, 20 inches in diameter.
Signed base, in four finishes.
The serial number is D 3053.

Floral design on a 20-inch-
diameter Copley shade
signed by C. Ladd.
Mahogany base, signed. The
serial number is C 3095.

Rare floral daisy design on a signed London shade, 9½ inches round. The base is signed, in four finishes. The serial number is 3042.

Opposite page:
Floral design with matching decorated and signed base with Springfield shade, signed, 16 inches in diameter. The serial number is D 3067.

Berkeley shade with Italian garden scene, signed, 16 inches in diameter. Signed base in two finishes. The serial number is D 3062.

Forest scene on a Berkeley shade, signed, 14 inches in diameter. The base is signed, in two finishes. The serial number is E 3055.

Farm scene with horse and buggy. Signed Exeter shade, 14 inches in diameter. The base is signed, in two finishes. The serial number is D 3025.

Piano lamp with tapestry
decoration on the signed
Mozart shade, ten inches
long. Signed base, in four
finishes. The serial number is
unknown.

Isabella scene on a nine-inch-wide signed Radcliffe shade. The base has various finishes and is signed. The serial number is C 3057.

Geometric design on a signed Wellsley shade, seven inches in diameter. Signed marble and silver-plate base. The serial number is E 3017.

Boudoir lamp featuring roses with black enamel outline on the exterior. Portsmouth shade, signed, eight inches wide. The base is signed and in two finishes. The serial number is B 3025.

Hexagonal lamp with floral decorations. Signed Bryn Mawr shade, seven inches in diameter. There are two finishes on the signed marble base. The serial number is B 7290.

Boudoir lamp with floral border on a signed Seville shade that is eight inches in diameter. The base is signed, in two finishes. The serial number is D 3073½.

Boudoir lamp with four panels, each one depicting one of the four seasons. Exeter shade, signed, eight inches in diameter. The base is signed and in two finishes. The serial number is 3047½.

Boudoir lamp with Garden of Allah scene on the signed Carlisle shade, eight inches in diameter. Signed base in two finishes. The serial number is 3047½.

Windmill-decorated boudoir lamp with a signed Carlisle shade, eight inches in diameter. The base is signed and in two finishes. The serial number is E 3055.

Italian garden scene boudoir lamp with a signed Lansdowne shade that is eight inches in diameter. Signed base in two finishes. The serial number is D 3056.

Floral decorated boudoir lamp with signed Vassar shade, six inches in diameter. Signed base in two finishes. The serial number is E 3018.

Galleons on a signed
Renaissance shade, four
inches in diameter.
Candelabra base, signed, in
two finishes. The serial
number is D 3094.

Parrots and floral border
decoration on a signed
Exeter shade, eight inches in
diameter. The base has two
finishes and is signed. The
serial number is D 3065.

Red poppy decoration on a signed Naushon shade, 7½ inches in diameter. The brass base is signed. The serial number is E 3043.

Four-sided Art Deco design on a signed Vassar shade, 6½ inches wide. Signed base in two finishes. The serial number is E 3018.

Stage coach decoration on a signed Nonquitt base, 5½ inches in diameter. Candle holder base in two finishes, signed. The serial number is E 3045.

Hexagonal lamp featuring signed Bryn Mawr shade with floral decorations. The shade is eight inches wide and the base is signed. The serial number is E 3033.

Early example of leaf design
with satin finish exterior.
Berlin shade, signed, ten
inches in diameter. Signed
base in two finishes. The
serial number is 3008.

Lacy design boudoir lamp
with a signed Lansdowne
shade, eight inches in
diameter. There are two
finishes on the signed base.
The serial number is D 3022.

Early example with glass chimney and green grapes and leaves. Nauseti shade, signed, with white matte finish, 12 inches in diameter. The brass base is signed; the serial number is E 3052.

Floral decorated signed fairy lamps with Coralline exterior. The shades are four inches in diameter. Matching glass bases, signed. The serial number is unknown.

Floor Lamp

Garden of Allah scene floor lamp with Carlisle shade, signed, 20 inches in diameter. Mahogany base, signed. The serial number is D 3095½.

Poppy decoration with blossoms and bird decoration, both on removable panels set in base. Radio lamp shade, signed, six inches high. The base is signed and in two finishes. The serial number is E 3036.

Butterflies and spiderweb on removable panel set in base. Radio lamp shade, signed, eight inches high. The base is signed and in two finishes. The serial number is E 3037.

Ship at sea scene on an octagonal Radio lamp shade, eight inches high. The base has two finishes and is signed. The serial number is E 3035.

Chandeliers

Ceiling chandelier with brass chains and fixture featuring Wedgwood decoration with white enamel outline on the exterior. Vienna shade, signed, 14 inches in diameter. The serial number is unknown.

Opposite page:
Ceiling chandelier hanging on brass chains and fixture, with red rose decoration and white enamel outline on the exterior. Signed Vienna shade, 14 inches in diameter. The serial number is unknown.

151

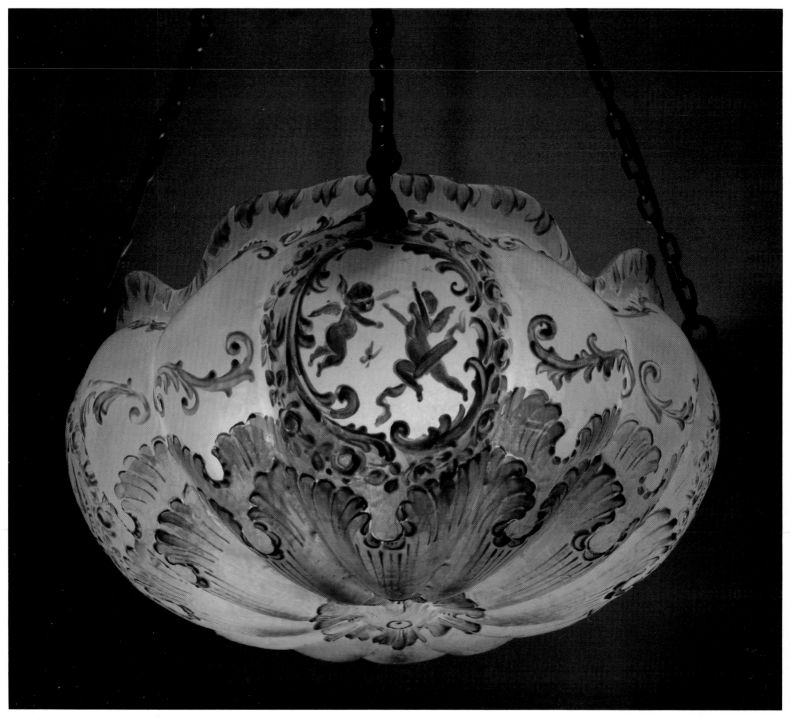

Ceiling chandelier with brass
chains and fixture featuring
cherub decoration on a pink
background and white
enamel outline on the
exterior. Signed 12-inch-
diameter Venice shade. The
serial number is unknown.

Opposite page:
Ceiling chandelier hanging
on brass chains and fixture
featuring dragonfly
decoration. Lucca shade,
signed, 12 inches in diameter.
The serial number is
unknown.

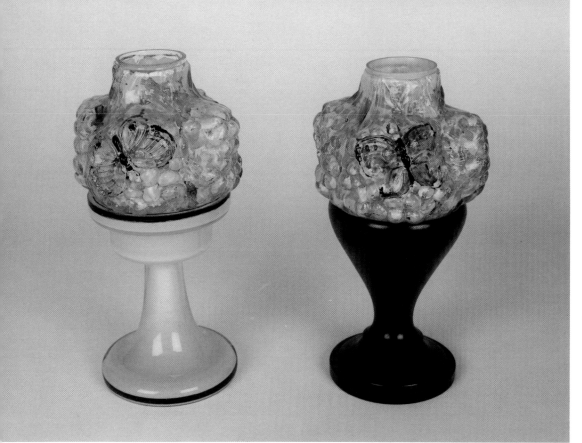

Puffy candle lamps with flora and fauna on a signed Butterfly and Lilacs shade, three inches in diameter. The base on the left is glass and the one on the right is mahogany; both are three inches in diameter. The serial number is unknown.

Puffy miniature nonelectrified candle lamp on double candelabra base. The signed Poppy shade is three inches in diameter; the brass base is signed. The serial number is C 6113.

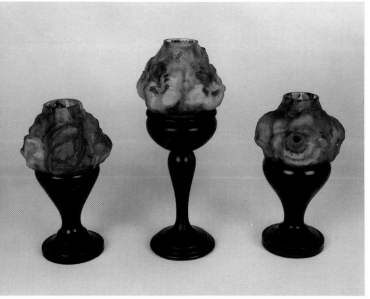

Puffy miniature candle lamps with roses and pansies. Signed Floral shade, three inches in diameter. The lamp has a mahogany base; the serial number is unknown.

Six floral panels set in brass
Panel shade, signed, 14
inches in diameter. The base
is in three finishes and
signed. The serial number is
B 3032.

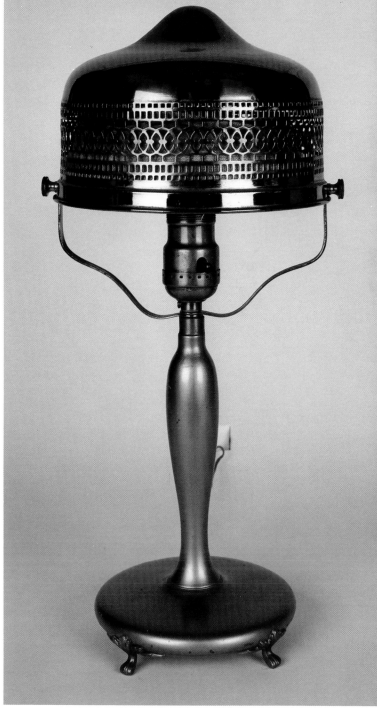

Brass and pierced-silk-lined
brass shade, signed, seven
inches in diameter. The base
is made of brass and signed.
The serial number is 3047½.

Ads

Pairpoint lamp advertisements from *Jewelers Circular Weekly*, September 5, 1929 and November 1930. Pairpoint styles were as diverse as they were beautiful.

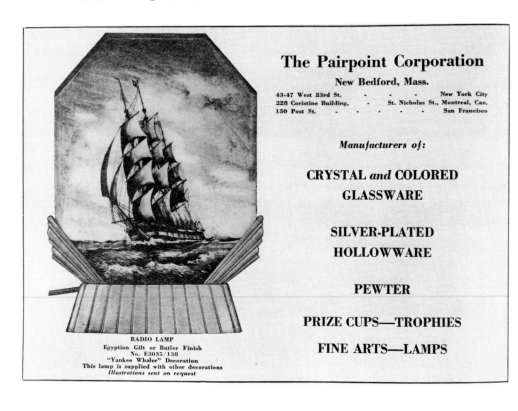

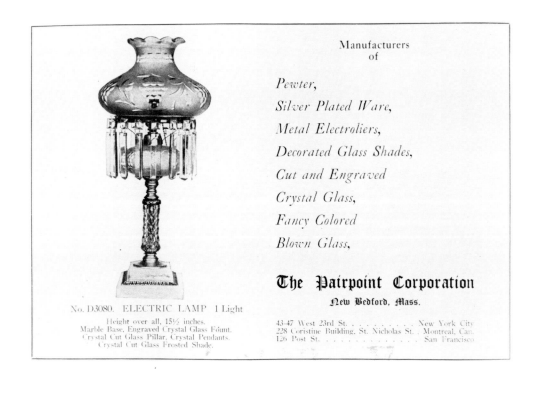

Opposite page:
Pairpoint lamp catalog pages, circa 1910.

OLD BRASS, EGYPTIAN BRASS, FLEMISH AND ANTIQUE FINISH.

OLD BRASS, EGYPTIAN BRASS, FLEMISH, ANTIQUE AND BRONZE FINISH.

OLD BRASS, EGYPTIAN BRASS, FLEMISH, ANTIQUE, BRONZE AND BUTLER FINISH.

OLD BRASS, EGYPTIAN BRASS, FLEMISH, ANTIQUE AND BRONZE FINISH.

EGYPTIAN BRASS AND BUTLER FINISH.

OLD BRASS, EGYPTIAN BRASS, FLEMISH, ANTIQUE AND BRONZE FINISH.

OLD BRASS, EGYPTIAN BRASS, FLEMISH, ANTIQUE AND BRONZE FINISH.

BUTLER, EGYPTIAN BRASS, OR FLEMISH FINISH.

EGYPTIAN BRASS AND BUTLER FINISH.

OLD BRASS, EGYPTIAN BRASS, FLEMISH, ANTIQUE, BRONZE AND BUTLER FINISH.

BUTLER, EGYPTIAN BRASS, OR FLEMISH FINISH.

ELECTRIC LAMP, 3 LIGHT.

BUTLER, EGYPTIAN BRASS, OLD BRASS OR FLEMISH FINISH.

OLD BRASS, EGYPTIAN BRASS, FLEMISH, ANTIQUE AND BUTLER FINISH.

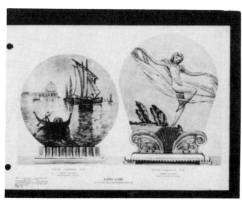

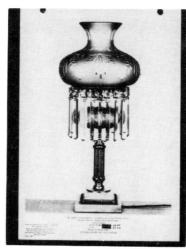

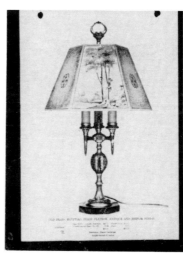

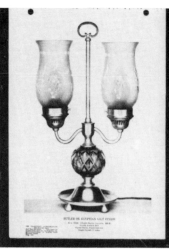

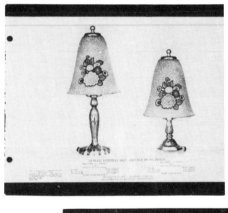

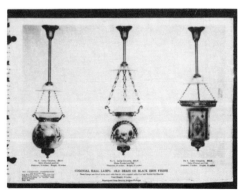

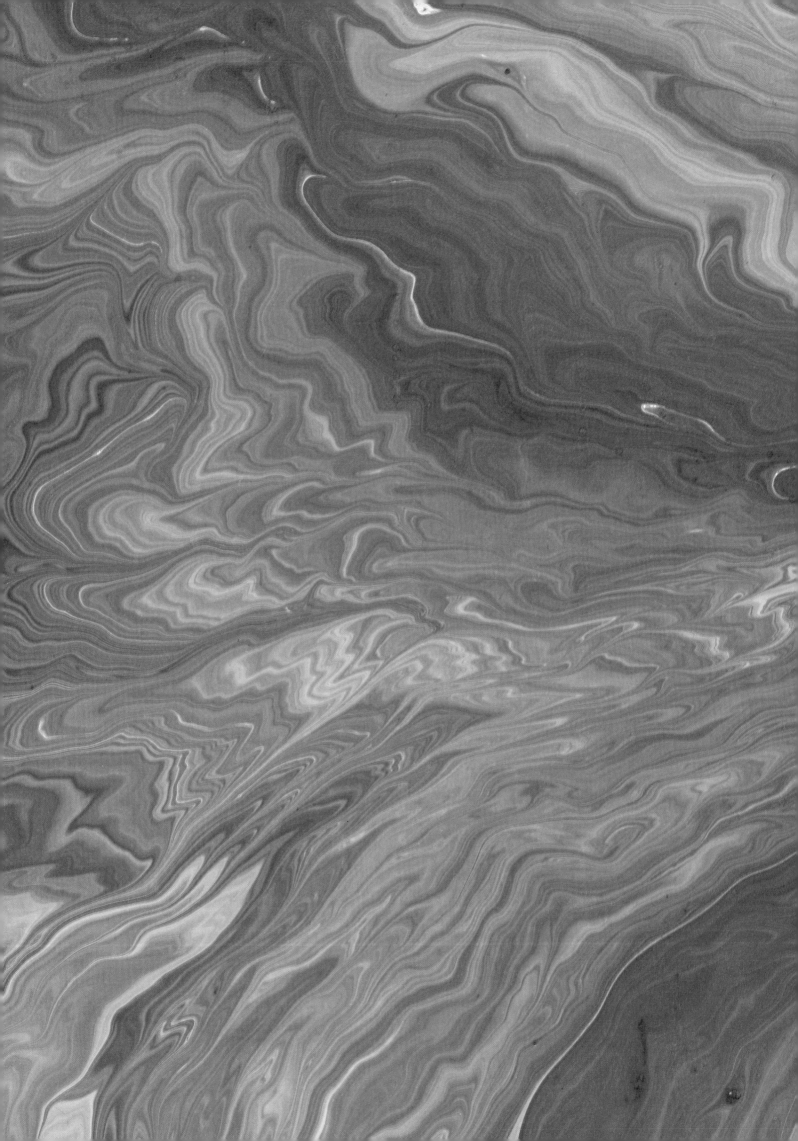